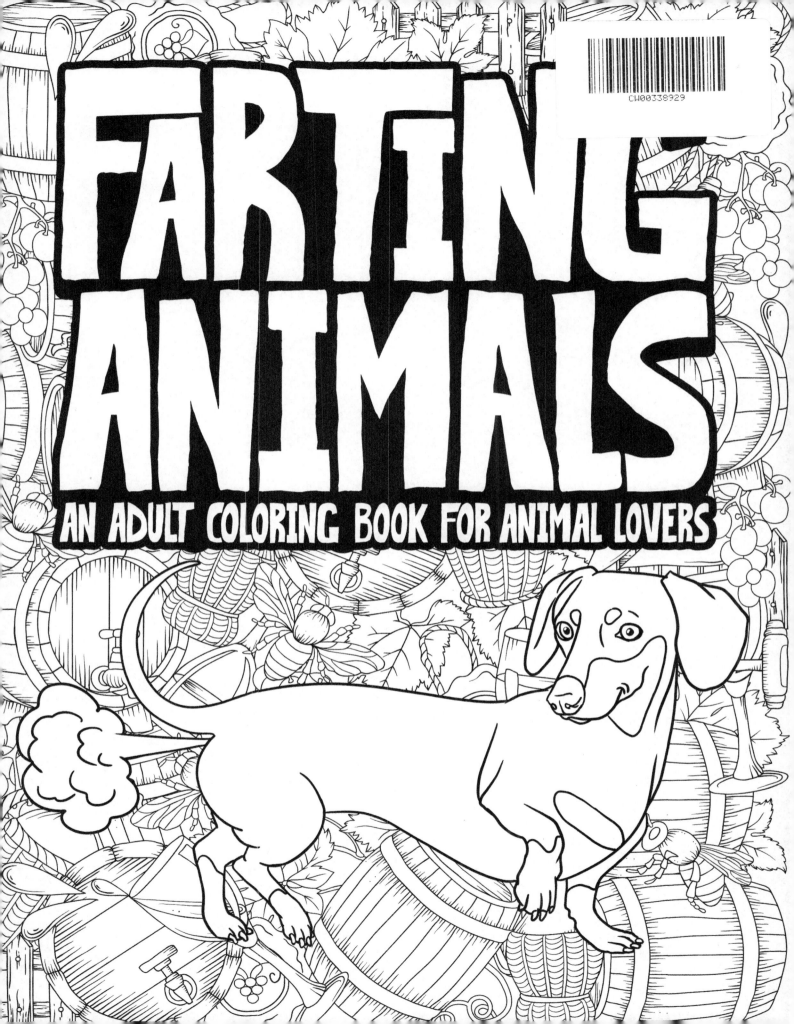

Want free goodies?
Email us at freebies@honeybadgercoloring.com

@honeybadgercoloring

Honey Badger Coloring

Shop our other books at
www.honeybadgercoloring.com

For questions and customer service, email us at
support@honeybadgercoloring.com

COLOR TEST PAGE

Llamas can spit 10 feet.

Sloths poop 1/3 their body weight each time they defecate.

Unicorns fart glitter.

Orangutans give birth every 8 years.

Hedgehogs are immune to most
snake venoms.

Foxes use the earth's magnetic field to help them hunt.

Dragons fart FIRE.

Honey badgers have a reversible anus.

Cats bring you their kill because they think you are an incompetent hunter.

Goats can develop different accents.

Sheep have rectangular pupils.

Female racoons have one partner, while males have many.

A mouse pregnancy lasts about 20 days.

Squirrels can jump 20 feet.

Some parrots can live up to 80 years.

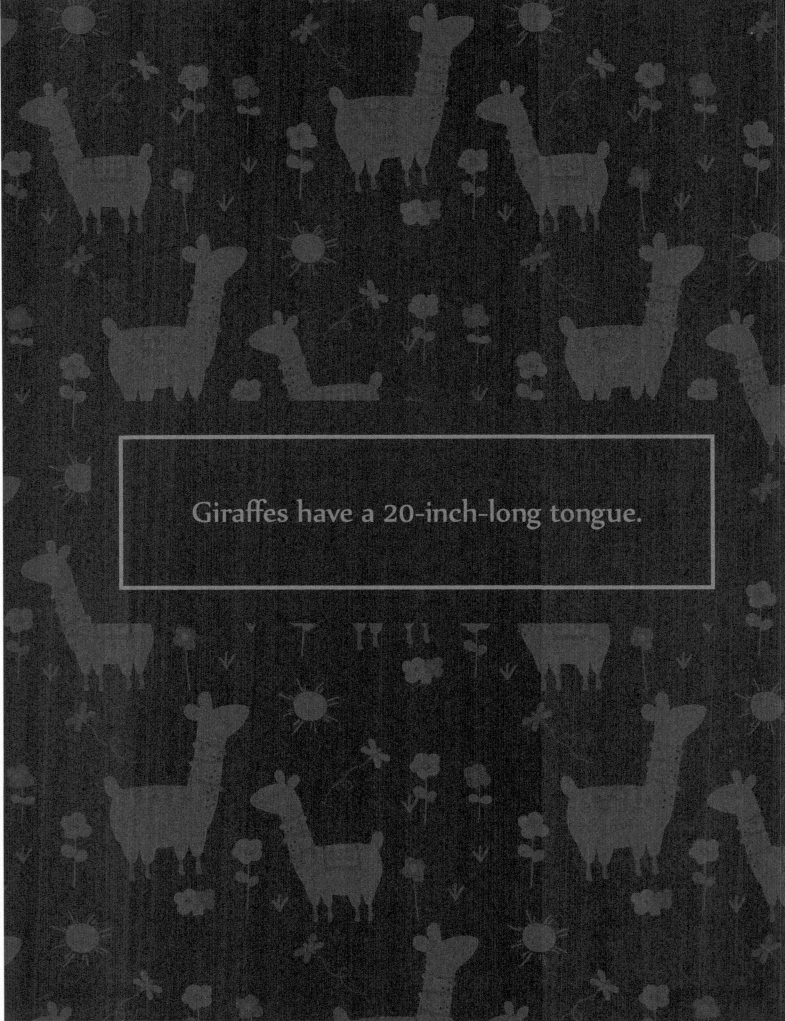

Giraffes have a 20-inch-long tongue.

Elephants can recognize themselves
in a mirror.

A tyrannosaurus rex had 50-60
BANANA-sized teeth.

Triceratops had nearly 800 teeth.

Platypuses breastfeed, but don't
have nipples.

Bears do not urinate during hibernation.

Belugas can mimic human speech.

Ducks do not have blood vessels or nerves in their feet.

Pandas eat 30 pounds of bamboo a day!

Koalas sleep up to 20 hours a day.

Narwhals cannot be successfully kept
in captivity. Their tusks can reach
10 feet long.

Pigs are smarter than dogs.

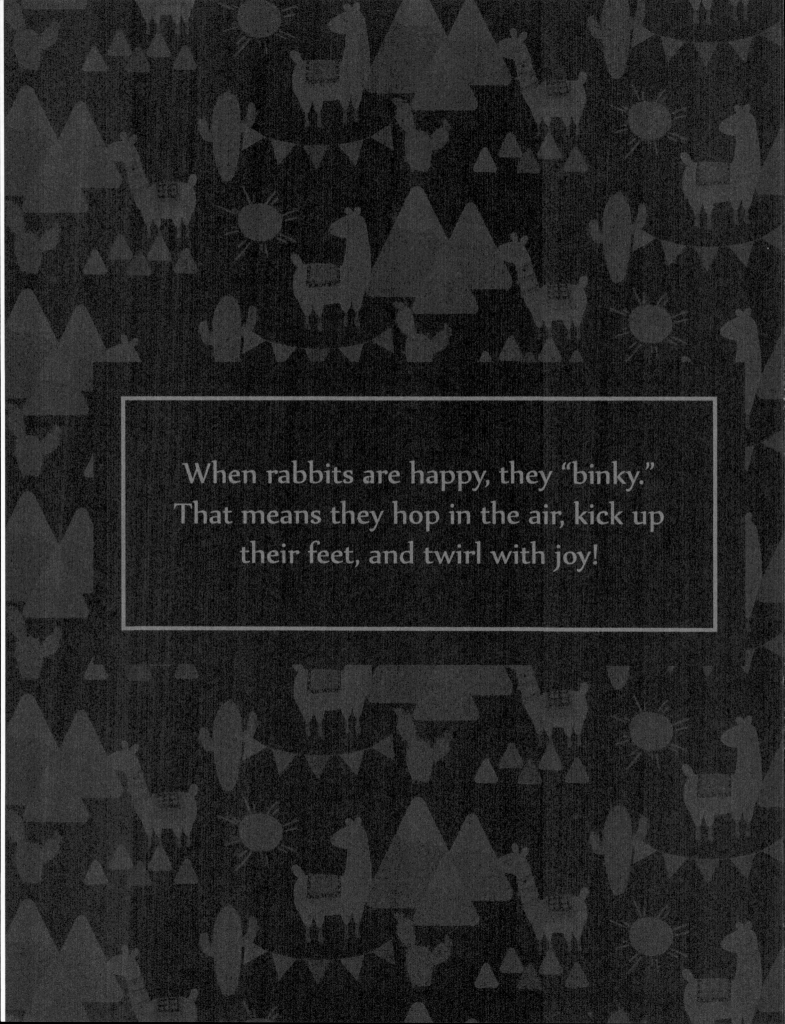

When rabbits are happy, they "binky."
That means they hop in the air, kick up
their feet, and twirl with joy!

Penguins mate for life.

Dachshunds were bred to hunt badgers.

Printed in Great Britain
by Amazon